Concrete
Dollars and Cents
Poems

Matthew Stolte

Concrete Dollars and Cents Poems by Matthew Stolte

ISBN: 978-1-7353850-0-6
1st Edition ISBN: 978-0-578-05164-2

Some of these poems first appeared in: *Score, Lost and Found Times* and *Pense Aqui*.

Second Edition

eMTeVisPub

http://www.lulu.com/spotlight/emtevispub
https://www.freewebs.com/matthewstolte/

This book was made possible in part by a generous grant from Dane Arts.

DANE ARTS

Engage. Connect. Inspire.

"Everybody's paying top dollar for scraps of paper, refrigerator doors - anything with a SAMO tag on it." - from the film *Basquiat*

"Cause you can't, you won't, and you don't stop" - from the song "Sure Shot" by Beastie Boys

"'I spent a few bucks. Top dollar. Who gives a shit?" - from the film *Casino*

"If we cannot stop, we cannot have insight."

"Nothing has a separate existence or a separate self. Everything has to inter-be with everything else." - Thich Nhat Hanh

"I've got dollars – I've got sense
wonder where the Third World went" – from the song "Video Crime" by David Bowie

"We are the dollars and cents and the pounds and pence (quiet down)
And the mark and the yen, and yeah
We're gonna crack your little souls (why don't you quiet down?)" – from the song "Dollars and Cents" by Radiohead

"...the polysemic champion must be *set*." – from *The Mother Tongue* by Bill Bryson

for Jean-Michel Basquiat

Forward by C. Mehrl Bennett

Concrete $ & ¢ Poems by Matthew T. Stolte
- First edition published 2010; Second edition published 2020 by eMTeVisPub
http://www.lulu.com/spotlight/emtevispub

Full discloser – I've known Matthew Stolte (Madison WI) for over 15 years, because of common associates in the field of visual poetry and the mail art network. Members of one side of my family lived in Madison and members of the other side lived in NE Iowa, close to Iowa's border with Wisconsin. As my spouse and I, or just myself, traveled from Ohio through the Midwest to visit family, Madison and consequently, Matthew Stolte, often are included in our itinerary. I first met Matthew in person when he issued an invitation in 2009 for artists to join him in exhibiting art/visual poetry in his studio as part of a city-wide event that included his studio, and I took him up on his offer with a carload of framed pieces. We used the opportunity to create collaborative paintings or collage as we waited for the public to show up, incorporating text using stencils, stamps, and collage. I enjoyed perusing Matthew's library of books by concrete and visual poets, which he continues to expand; and he had started a micro press under the imprint eMTeVisPub for Avant poetry. mIEKAL aND, a former resident of Madison who now lives in rural Wisconsin in the 'Driftless Zone' (a geological and very poetic term concerning land carved out by glaciers) offered his Xexoxial Editions books for sale during this event. Matthew and mIEKAL would travel to Columbus OH the following year for The Ohio State Univ.'s Avant Writing Symposium, so we also met on our home ground. We still exchange mail art on occasion. Some background info about Matthew and the year Concrete $ & ¢ Poems was first published: The largest oil spill in U.S. history occurred in 2010 when an explosion of the Deepwater Horizon oil rig released 210 million gallons of oil meant for BP into the Gulf of Mexico, impacting over 1000 miles of shoreline from Texas to Florida and killing thousands of sea birds and marine creatures. It was 85 days before the leak was capped. This made a huge long-lasting environmental impact, and there have been other medium sized and smaller oil spill accidents in U.S. waters before and after that event. Matthew has a deep understanding and concern for the negative impact human greed has on global marine life and our environment in general. That may explain the frequent appearance in his concrete poetry of words like SHELL and SEA, and his use of $ & ¢ symbols for capital 'S' & 'c' as symbols of human greed and its impact on our natural environment.

Today, in this time of Trump rollbacks of environmental protections for the sake of big business and his dismantling of the EPA's effective leadership, regulatory efforts, and effectiveness, this book deserves another look. So it is fortuitous that Matthew has released an expanded second edition! Matthew's introduction for Concrete $ & ¢ Poems helpfully explains various methods of approaching these poems. Words appear as sparse, separated words in large font on each page, but with close and varied readings these words easily morph into phrases, separated or connected. In my first reading, I used my own cognizance to puzzle out the text/symbols; but in subsequent readings I made an effort to follow the author's introductory hints, which helped enrich the phrases that developed in my thoughts/interpretations. It's all part of finding out where our real life concerns and the author's literary/poetic/artistic output converge. Matthew Stolte's hopes to help better this world in which we live are viscerally made evident in the process of reading this book. But also I feel that the creative way in which he approaches 'poetry' is a literary reward in itself.
-- C. Mehrl Bennett / November 2019

Introduction to the 2nd Edition

Description of $ & ¢ Poems

Dollars and Cents poems have at least a triple reading, not just two as is frequent in advertising. For example, the substitution of the $ for the letter "S" in the word *sale* ($ale) would only make sense as an advertisement for beer. There is the whole "S" or "C" word without the value added & the shortened word after the value is added, both words in conjunction with the idea of value.

Further interpretations of $ & ¢ poems include noting punctuation & foreign words as well as reading the bars through the $ & ¢ signs as the capital I or miniscule l. Note sometimes letters are symbols, e.g. "O" for Sun, "D" for ½ moon. For the most part, personal names, plurals & complete variations have been left out of this collection. Poems akin to pwoermds have not been left out at the author's caprice.

I cite 2 examples of this construction from concrete literature. Ian Lee's "the medium" from the book *The Third Wor*d War,* in which a stenograph card rests on a stereoscope viewer, was brought to my attention by the concrete poet Endwar (Andrew Russ). The card reads "I" on the left side & "S" on the right, reading "IS", which would read as $ as seen through the stereoscope.

d.a. Levy's *The Tibetan Stroboscope* makes use of the $ at the very end, in the word Stroboscope, which is split in two & the $ used in place of the 2nd "S". This reads "$cope", likely intended to read both scope & cope. The word "U.$.$.A." also appears at the beginning of the work.

I believe my 1st $s & ¢s poem was "$top", inspired by the film *Basquiat*. As new poems arose, I employed them directly to canvas in paintings. At some point I started collecting them separately. All of the poems were written from overheard speech (dates & contextual references were initially noted but most were later discarded). I never wrote a poem from browsing the dictionary, considering possibilities.

Continuing to think of new poems the process became involuntary. Every "S" or "C" word (or related) I heard underwent consideration as a possible poem. This obsession lasted approximately 2 years, when the bulk of these poems were written. I also interpreted the poems as such when overheard, adding alternative meanings to what was being said.

All of the poems are meditations on interrelatedness, or as the Vietnamese poet Buddhist monk, Thich Nhat Hanh, puts it, "interbeing". The poem "$top", originally intended to convey solely an economic meaning, additionally acquired the Buddhist idea of "stopping".

I often include several $s & ¢s poems together in "oil spill" or environmental themed paintings & visual poems. Poems such as: $ea, $oil, & $hell. "Poem for the Oceans" appeared on the back cover of the 1st edition.

Poem for the Oceans

$ea $eve$$ $ea ¢eve¢$
$ea ¢eve¢$ $ea ¢eve$$
$ea eve $ea ¢eve¢
$ea $eve¢ $ea ¢eve$
$oil s$ick $oil s¢ick
$ea $oil ¢rude
i.¢e. ea $pill $hell
$till $port $pine
$$ick $ea s$ick
$¢ick $ea s¢ick
$pill$ $¢amp$
$pills $¢amp¢
s¢ick s$ick
$ail $ale
$oiled car.pet
¢loud car.p
$quid
$quid pro quo
eahell
eahell$

Two poems from the original collection have been omitted, one changed, & fifty-four new poems added.

Many Thanks to Paul Schultz for his editorial skill in shaping the introductions for both the 1st & 2nd editions of this book.

Many Thanks to C. Mehrl Bennett for her generous forward, when I merely solicited a blurb.

A Note on the COVID-19 Pandemic

I planned on publishing this edition in March 2020 – midway through the month the COVID-19 pandemic hit Wisconsin. After working 3 weeks during the crisis I lost my job & joined the more than 40 million Americans who filed for unemployment by the end of May. With newfound time & a generous grant from Dane Arts I was able to publish.

It is in the same spirit of the interconnectedness of all things both before & after the emergence of COVID-19 that this expanded & more accessible edition manifests.

Many Thanks to Dane Arts.

$o

i$

$a

u$

a$$

¢OD

i.¢e.

i¢i

$ad

$ax

$ea

$et

$eu

$ex

$he

$in

$it

$ot

$un

¢age

¢a.$m.

¢a.¢m.

¢are

¢a$h

¢ash

¢her

¢how

¢lit

¢o¢k

¢ode

¢old

¢one

¢o$t

¢raw

Di.¢e.

fee$

fee¢

he$$

he¢¢

me$$

NEW$

$age

$aid

$ail

$ale

$and

$ave

$car

$¢a.m.

$cum

ea

$ear

$eat

$end

$hoe

$hop

$ilk

$$a.m.

$lip

$low

$lug

$$ug

$mug

$now

$oil

$oft

$old

oo

$our

$par

$paz

$pin

$tab

$tar

$top

W$NE

a$one

a¢one

¢anal

¢heap

¢lean

¢lick

¢lock

¢loud

¢lout

¢over

¢raft

¢ream

¢reek

¢rest

¢rude

¢rush

look$

$over

$aint

AAD

$A¢AD

$ales

$¢ad$

$¢ale

car

$cope

$¢rum

$¢our

$elle

$even

$have

$hell

hoe

$hoot

hot

$i$$y

$kill

$lake

$lips

$lush

$mall

$melt

$o¢k$

ON¢

$ON¢¢

$pace

$pare

$park

$peak

$pear

$perm

$pies

$pill

$pine

$poke

$punk

$quad

$tale

$tank

$teak

$teal

$till

$tock

$tone

$trip

$tuck

$urge

$ward

$warm

$we$$

$WI$$

$will

$wine

$word

y¢o

¢enter

¢hubby

¢lo$ed

¢off.e.e

¿como?

¢over$

¢RUT¢H

e$¢ape

ex¢use

oi$eau

$ample

$¢AMP$

$¢AMP¢

$¢rape

$ea i.¢e.

$hovel

$inner

$kill$

$often

$oiled

$on.net

$paced

$table

$toLTE

$toned

$train

unet

$upper

a$$hole

big $oil

¢an$wer

¢heated

¢$utter

¢¢utter

¢our.age

¢ulture

MON$TER

$killed

$mitten

$toning

$topped

$uppers

$upper$

top$oil

$ea eve

$ea ¢eve¢

$ea $eve¢

$ea ¢eve$

ea¢ape

eahell

$ea s$ick

$ea s¢ick

$hopping

$pill.age

topoil

$trainer

$trapped

$warming

¢are.fully

¢rude $oil

hard$hell

eahell$

$laughter

$paced out

$peak $oil

WI$¢on$in

$ample me$$

hoe & $o¢k$

$quid pro quo

Suggestions for Further Reading

Ampersand Squared: an/thology of pwoermds – edited by Geof Huth –
Runaway Spoon Press 2004

Anthology Spidertangle – edited by mIEKAL aND – Xexoxial Editions 2009

Basquiat: a quick killing in art – by Phoebe Hoban – Viking Penguin 1998

The Heart of the Buddha's Teaching – by Thich Nhat Hanh – Broadway Books
edition 1999

Lost & Found Times No. 52 – June 2004 – edited by John M. Bennett –
consultant C. Mehrl Bennett

The Mother Tongue: English & How It Got That Way – by Bill Bryson –
William Morrow and Company Inc. 1990

Score 19 - Edited by Crag Hill

Texistence – by Geof Huth & mIEKAL aND – Xerox Sutra Editions 2008

Third Wor*d War – by Ian Lee – A & W Publishers Inc. 1978

The Tibetan Stroboscope – by d.a. Levy – Quixote 1968